Praise for *You Are the Mother of All Mothers:*

"Inspiring and heartfelt."

~ PUBSLUSH.COM

"*You Are the Mother of All Mothers* is a rare glimpse into the broken heart of the bereaved mother. Angela's words gently offer freedom from misplaced blame and are a brave invitation to embrace peace, joy, and wholehearted living once again."

~ CHRISTINA RASMUSSEN, AUTHOR OF *SECOND FIRSTS*

"*You Are the Mother of All Mothers* is a refreshingly honest portrayal of a mother's undying love for her child."

~ SEAN HANISH, WRITER/PRODUCER/DIRECTOR OF *RETURN TO ZERO*

"Healing, empowering, and deeply moving. A must-read for bereaved mothers everywhere."

~ DR. GLORIA HORSLEY AND DR. HEIDI HORSLEY, INTERNATIONAL GRIEF EXPERTS AND FOUNDERS OF THE OPEN TO HOPE FOUNDATION

"Angela has been to hell and back, and she wrote this moving and inspiring book so that others will not have to journey alone."

~ WILLIAM J. DOHERTY, PH.D., PROFESSOR OF FAMILY SOCIAL SCIENCE AT THE UNIVERSITY OF MINNESOTA AND AUTHOR OF *TAKE BACK YOUR MARRIAGE*

"Angela encourages mothers not to let guilt and shame define them, despite their natural tendencies to have these feelings."

~ SHEROKEE ILSE, BEREAVED MOTHER AND AUTHOR OF *EMPTY ARMS: COPING WITH MISCARRIAGE, STILLBIRTH AND NEONATAL DEATH*

"With her honest and forthright sentiment, bereaved mothers everywhere can find a friend, confidant, and fellow survivor in Angela."

~ LORI MULLINS ENNIS, EDITOR OF *STILL STANDING MAGAZINE*

"You Are the Mother of All Mothers" is a lighthouse in the stormy sea of a bereaved mother's grief. Angela's words not only light the way, they heal."

~ KELLY MCDYRE, EXECUTIVE DIRECTOR OF FAITH'S LODGE

"Angela offers fierce encouragement, reminding women of their superhero nature, given the invincible strength it takes to mother a child they can no longer hold, see, touch, or hear."

~ RACHEL AWES, PSYCHOLOGIST, AUTHOR + ART PLAYGROUNDIST AT RACHELAWES.COM

"Passionate, searing, and unapologetic, Angela bares our resilient capacity to embrace the seemingly impossible alchemy of profound grief, life, and love."

~ CHARLOTTE GRACE, PSY.D., CLINICAL PSYCHOLOGIST

"You Are the Mother of All Mothers" comforts the tender heart. Angela's deeply authentic voice is one of a dear friend offering inspiration and care."

~ MIA BOLTE, M.A., BUDDHIST PSYCHOTHERAPIST

"This book will act as a hand reaching out to people in their darkest time."

~ CATHERINE HEWSON AND DR. MAIBRITT PEDERSEN ZARI, FOUNDERS OF *FOREVER PRESENT A GIFT FROM PEMA AND ISLA*

"Angela steps right inside grief to allow something beautiful to grow and shows us that we can too."

~ STACEY GRIPSHOVER, FOUNDER OF RAISING BLUE

YOU ARE THE Mother OF ALL Mothers

a MESSAGE of HOPE for the GRIEVING HEART

Angela Miller

WISE Ink
CREATIVE + PUBLISHING

Copyright © 2014 by Angela Miller

All rights reserved. No part of this book may be reproduced, scanned, or distributed in any printed or electronic form without permission from the publisher; exceptions are made for brief excerpts used in published reviews. Please do not participate in or encourage piracy of copyrighted materials in violation of the author's rights. Purchase only authorized editions.

ISBN 13: 978-1-940014-19-7
Library of Congress Number: 2014938082

Printed in Canada

18 17 16 15 14   5 4 3 2 1

Art & hand lettering by Franchesca Cox
Book Design by Mayfly Design
Typeset in Bernhard Modern Std

Published by Wise Ink Creative Publishing
Minneapolis, Minnesota
www.wiseinkpub.com

To order, visit **ABedForMyHeart.com**. Reseller discounts available.

Para Noah, el latido de mi corazón.
For Noah, my heartbeat.

There are few books that address the weight of guilt and shame that a grieving mother carries after the loss of her child. The deep feeling of failure that accompanies child loss can cripple the heart, mind, and soul. Reengaging in life after loss and attempting to find hope again is an ongoing battle—one no bereaved mother should fight alone.

No matter the age or cause of death, no matter the story, this book is for you, sweet mama.

This is the book you can reach for in the middle of the night when you feel like no one understands your pain. It's the book you can carry with you any time, anywhere, to give you a lift of hope, a sliver of light in the darkness. It's a balm for your broken heart, a comfort for your aching soul, an elixir for those feelings of guilt. It's an invitation to replace the insidious lies with a truth that will resonate with all your broken pieces, a truth that will sink deep into your bones. It's a way to lift your heart again and again with some gentle, loving encouragement from someone who knows.

Whether today or years from now—someday, somehow—I hope you know what I know to be true:

You truly are the mother of all mothers—a warrior mama through and through.

I have to tell you this.

. . .

You didn't fail. Not even a little.

You are *not*
a horrible mother.

. . .

You didn't choose this.
You didn't *want* this to happen.
You didn't do anything *wrong*.

It just happened. *To you.*

. . .

Despite your begging, pleading, praying,
hoping against all hope it would not.
Even though everything within you
was screaming *no, no, no, no, no.*

. . .

God didn't do this to punish you, smite you,
or to teach you a lesson. That is not God's way.

That is not God's way.

. . .

You could not have prevented this if you tried harder,
prayed harder, or were a "better" person.

. . .

Nor if you ate better, loved harder, yoga-ed more, did x, y, or z to the *n*th degree—fill in the blank with any other lie your mind devises.

You could not have prevented this even if you could have predicted the future like *no one can*.

. . .

No, there is nothing more you could have done.
You did everything you possibly could have.

to choose the pain all over again

. . .

And you are the best mother there is because you would have done absolutely anything to keep your child alive. To breathe your last breath instead. To choose the pain all over again just to spend one more minute together.

That is the ultimate
kind of love. You are
the *ultimate* kind of mother.

. . .

So wash your hands of any naysayers, betrayers, or those who sprinted in the other direction when you needed them most. Wash your hands of the people who may have falsely judged you, ostracized you, or stigmatized you because of what happened to you. Wash your hands of anyone who has made you feel *less than* by questioning everything you did or didn't do. Anyone whose words or looks have implied this was somehow your fault.

. . .

This was *not* your fault.
This will *never* be your fault,
no matter how many different ways
someone tries to tell you it was.

. . .

Especially if that *someone* happens to be you. Sometimes it's not what others are saying that keeps you shackled in shame. Sometimes you adopt others' misguided opinions and assumptions.

. . .

Sometimes it's your own inner voice that shoves you into the darkest corner of despair, like an abuser, telling you over and over and over again you failed as a mother. Convincing you *if only* this and *what if* that, it never would have happened. Saying you *coulda, shoulda* done this or that so your child would not have died.

...

That is a lie of the sickest kind. Do not believe it, not even for a second. Do not let it sink into your bones. Do not let it smother that beautiful, beautiful light of yours.

Instead, breathe in this truth
with every part of yourself:
*You are the best damn
mother in the entire world.*

No one else could do what you do.

. . .

No one else could do what you do.

. . .

No one else could ever mother your child
as well as you can, as well as you are.

No one else could let your
child's love and light shine
through the way you do.

No one else could mother
your dead child as bravely.

No one else could carry this unrelenting burden as courageously.

. . .

No one else could carry this unrelenting burden as courageously. It is the heaviest, most torturous burden there is.

...

There is no one, no one, no one who could *ever*, ever replace you. *No one.*

. . .

You were chosen to be your child's mother. Yes—*chosen*. And no one could parent your child better in life or in death than you do.

You have within you
a sacred strength.

. . .

You are the mother of *all* mothers.

. . .

So breathe, mama, keep *breathing*. Believe, mama, keep *believing*. Fight, mama, keep *fighting* for this truth to uproot the lies in your heart—you didn't fail. Not even a little.

For whatever it's worth,
I see you.

. . .

I hear your guttural sobs. I feel your ache deep inside my bones. And it doesn't make me uncomfortable to put my fingers as a makeshift Band-Aid over the gaping hole in your heart until the scabs come, if and when they do.

. . .

It takes invincible strength to mother a child
you can no longer *hold, see, touch,* or *hear*.
You are a superhero mama.

. . .

I see you fall down and get up, fall down
and get up, over and over again. I notice the grit
and guts it takes to pry yourself out of bed
every single day and force your bloodied
feet to stand up and keep walking.

. . .

I see you walking this path of life you've been given,
where every breath and step apart from your child is a
physical, emotional, and spiritual battleground.
A fight for your own survival.
A fight to quiet the insidious lies.

But the truth is,
you haven't failed at all.
In fact, it's quite
the opposite.

But the truth is you haven't failed at all.

you are the mother of all mothers

. . .

You are the mother of *all* mothers.

. . .

Truly, the most *inspiring, courageous, loving* mother there is—a warrior mama through and through.

Truly the most inspiring, courageous, loving mother there is — a warrior mama through and through.

For even in death, you lovingly mother your precious child still.

Thank you to my husband, Rob, the love of my life. You lent me your courage until I could find my own again, and you dared to believe in me when no one else did. Your love breathed me back to life. Without you, so many beautiful miracles, including this book, wouldn't exist.

Thank you to my three children for being the beautiful souls you are. I love you beyond any words, in any language, in the history of ever.

Thank you Jenny, Charlotte, and Mia who graciously saved my life and still are.

Thank you Jacinta, Beth, Amy, Hannah, Krista, Jessica, Kelly, Cathy, Marie, Tara, Jess, Erin, Kay, Emily, Sami, Kerry, Cheryl, Katie, and Gwen, who embody the true essence of loving friendship.

Thank you to all my Pubslush supporters, especially Emily & Eric, who enthusiastically rallied behind this mission of love, and implicitly trusted my vision. Your support is what made this book both possible and gorgeous in every way.

Thank you to my editor, Angela Wiechmann, whose first words about this book were: "Some people write from the heart, and some people write from the soul, but this is written from a place even deeper than that—a place I didn't even know existed." You edited this book from that very same place.

Thank you, Ryan Scheife of Mayfly Design, for your artistic vision, impeccable design, and unending dedication.

Thank you, Franchesca Cox, for the gorgeous custom art and hand lettering that made this book more beautiful than I ever dreamed possible.

Thank you to my publishers, Amy Quale and Dara Beevas of Wise Ink Creative Publishing, for wholeheartedly believing in me and my book every step of the way.

And a deep bow of gratitude to all who picked me up from the gutter on a stretcher of love. Your love is what saved me and what is saving me still.

"I wish I could show you, when you are lonely or in darkness, the astonishing light of your own being."

~ Hafiz

In Loving Memory of...

Abigaile Grace Christenson
Alyssa Elizabeth Hagen
Alyssa Grace Divers
Annabella Jane Sterk
Antoinette Maree Watts
Asher Eugene Allen
Avery Minnie LaBreche-Olson
Boston Ryan Schwamberger
Bram Xavier Venn
Brantley Matthew Begosh
Brinly Joy Benson
Caleb Alexander Wilson
Cameryn Barnhart
Chandler William Mario DaSilva
Chris Seehuetter
Conley David Heidenreich
Connor Scott Millard
Cooper Andrew Aikens
Cristopher Michael Castetter
Declan Black Carmical
Derek Robert Peterson
Dylan Bullock
Dylan Skye Goedeker
Emily Christine Carstensen

Ethan John Finne
Eve Morey
Faith Rose King
Gael Castillo Araya
Hannah Rose ZumMallen
Henry Alan Butler
Isabella Rose Otis
Isla Mere Hewson Baldwin
Jason Rawn Shively
Jenna Belle Cox
Jillian Alexis Crist
John Matthew and Alexander Trey Ennis
Jonathan Edward Sultan
Jordan Lee Woods
Joseph Robert Eschweiler
Jude Samuel Benson
Kiera Maurine Umlandt
Kristina "Nina" Westmoreland
Kyle and Mim Koenen
Leo Blue Bernard Gripshover
Liam Alexander Erion
Lily Ann Kresl
Lilyana Marie Auxier
Luke Alan Melius

Luna Williamson
Mason Thomas Stansbury
Milo Guy Richardson
Nash Adam Sievers
Noah Castillo Araya
Nora Norine-Kelly Henke
Parker James Dreyer
Quinn, April and Fiona Sedinger
Raelynne Kaya Rosa
River Daniel Wheeler
Robert "Penny" Disburg
Ryan Alexander Brune
Samuel Alexander Jeffers
Saphire Rayne Haughton
Sasha Marie McHale
Sebastian Xavier Ross
Shannon Edward Connett
Shaun Brian Johnson
Sophie Paige and Madigan Grace Lillard
Timothy Winston Clark
Travis Lee Boehle
Weston Eli Robbins
Xavier McKinley Trent

"I will carry you, here and there, there and here, until I am where you are."
~ Angela Miller

In Loving Memory of...

Abigaile Grace Christenson
Alyssa Elizabeth Hagen
Alyssa Grace Divers
Annabella Jane Sterk
Antoinette Maree Watts
Asher Eugene Allen
Avery Minnie LaBreche-Olson
Boston Ryan Schwamberger
Bram Xavier Venn
Brantley Matthew Begosh
Brinly Joy Benson
Caleb Alexander Wilson
Cameryn Barnhart
Chandler William Mario DaSilva
Chris Seebuetter
Conley David Heidenreich
Connor Scott Millard
Cooper Andrew Aikens
Cristopher Michael Castetter
Declan Black Carmical
Derek Robert Peterson
Dylan Bullock
Dylan Skye Goedeker
Emily Christine Carstensen

Ethan John Finne
Eve Morey
Faith Rose King
Gael Castillo Araya
Hannah Rose ZumMallen
Henry Alan Butler
Isabella Rose Otis
Isla Mere Hewson Baldwin
Jason Rawn Shively
Jenna Belle Cox
Jillian Alexis Crist
John Matthew and Alexander Trey Ennis
Jonathan Edward Sultan
Jordan Lee Woods
Joseph Robert Eschweiler
Jude Samuel Benson
Kiera Marine Umlandt
Kristina "Nina" Westmoreland
Kyle and Mim Koenen
Leo Blue Bernard Gripshover
Liam Alexander Erion
Lily Ann Kreal
Lilyana Marie Auxier
Luke Alan Melius

Luna Williamson
Mason Thomas Stansbury
Milo Guy Richardson
Nash Adam Sievers
Noah Castillo Araya
Nora Norine-Kelly Henke
Parker James Dreyer
Quinn, April and Fiona Sedinger
Raelynne Kaya Rosa
River Daniel Wheeler
Robert "Penny" Disburg
Ryan Alexander Brune
Samuel Alexander Jeffers
Saphire Rayne Haughton
Sasha Marie McHale
Sebastian Xavier Ross
Shannon Edward Connett
Shaun Brian Johnson
Sophie Paige and Madigan Grace Lillard
Timothy Winston Clark
Travis Lee Boehle
Weston Eli Robbins
Xavier McKinley Trent

"I will carry you, here and there, there and here, until I am where you are."
~Angela Miller

© Kerry Kresl

Angela Miller is a writer, survivor, and grief activist who empowers others to rediscover life after loss. She has garnered an international following through her candid writing about child loss and grief in *Still Standing Magazine* and elsewhere. She is the founder and facilitator of the grief support group *Bereaved Mamas* and the online community, ABedForMyHeart.com. *You Are the Mother of All Mothers* was originally written as a letter to herself and was later published as an essay in *Still Standing Magazine*. When she received an overwhelming international response, she knew her words had the ability to touch others on a grander scale. *You Are the Mother of All Mothers* is her first book, and is dedicated to bereaved mothers everywhere. Angela lives in Minnesota with her husband and two children.

Franchesca Cox is a creative soul living in South Texas. She is the author of *Celebrating Pregnancy Again* and journals life and holistic living tips on her blog, WildfeathersVintage.com.